The Keeper
and the Kept

The Keeper
and the Kept

Maurice B. Harris

To order additional copies of this book, contact:
Xlibris Corporation
1-888-795-4274
www.Xlibris.com
Orders@Xlibris.com
82223

Contents

Introduction 7

The Keeper and the Kept 19

Index 59

Introduction

When I first thought of writing, I could see my father. Strangely enough, I believe my father had as much influence on me writing this book as my dramatic experience. He was a quiet man, moving from the sharecropper's farms of Arkansas to the Midwest to make a better life for a family of six. My father came from a family of educators. With just an elementary education, he was considerably intelligent. I always had the idea that just getting by was good enough. My two sisters and my brother who had formal education encouraged me into getting a college education, especially after my sisters elevated my father's intelligence level to that of someone with a four-year college degree. My father loved to read and enjoyed books. I also loved books and was always fascinated with them. As a youth, I never had the patience to read and complete every book I picked up. Now I have a craving for knowledge and the behavior of man. When I began my career as a correctional officer, I sometimes would ask myself, Who are these men tossed into the pits of society in an unknown territory that has been uprooted from what is called a free and lawful society? I once walked hand in hand with them in what we call a healthy, humane world. I wonder what we think about hiding some of these horror stories and immoral acts of men locked behind bars are real as seen in the movies. The first ninety days are vital, all right, but to whom? I didn't know much about cultural shock in the prison system, but I was soon to find out.

When the iron doors close behind you and you enter into a world of disbelief, you try to look unafraid. You tell yourself, *I don't want to die in this place*. There's the fear of the unknown or what will happen next. You also feel ashamed and embarrassed thinking how many more men will come to live like animals. As I go through the daily mental torture of being locked in with men from all walks of life, some are vindictive, immoral, uneducated, not to mention racist. How will I ever become fair but firm in this system? I still wonder who's keeping whom. Once I learned to use and know the difference between psychology and prison psychology, my daily routine became a challenge. There is a time when a day's work is exciting, living on the edge, and then you realize the large amount of authority you have from time to time. I became very concerned. I recall the steady diet of name-calling that drove some officers to alcohol or drugs, even suicide, trying to distinguish the difference between the keeper and the kept. I was looking to gain respect, but you soon find out it's all about how you play the con game and that respect comes in time. It is very frightening to see a highly educated officer lured into introducing contraband into the system without even knowing it. I watched some inmates struggling to overcome the adversities of prison life, trying not to fall into the cracks of the swamps of society.

This environment brings some inmates to take their own lives, and the suicide rate is high among *marks, snitches, and scrubs. After a few days, you begin to understand why freedom is worth dying for. Hopefully, this book will be a deterrent for someone that is possibly heading down this road. To others, it could be a source of information to the unknown. Some state and federal laws allow inmates to dictate how he or she is addressed. What is the next step, Mr. Criminal? Who's keeping whom?

1. *Administrative segregation*—Where defenders are placed while waiting a court date for disciplinary action for policy violations or for their own protection.

2. *Aggie*—Hoe, a long-handled tool for cultivating or weeding.

3. *Ain't no dougt*—He knows what you are saying.

4. *Already*—Got it together, it's done.

5. *Back gate*—Rear of prison, rear entrance.

6. *Bitch-ass white boy*—Weak, like a woman.

7. *Break me off*—Give me something home boy.

8. *Bring it all back with you/witha/witcha*—What field officers say when they want field workers to clear all the waste they have chopped down.

9. *Cellblock*—Sleeping area for offenders.

10. *Blue Foot*—Weak male, new boot, drive up, new offender in the system.

11. *Bumping your gums*—Talking about things you know nothing about, just talking.

12. *Bump it on down*—Move from the spot you are standing, go away.

13. *Bust it up or open*—Open food, jack smack in a can, open a can of food.

14. *Bust you up*—Going to hurt you or fight, inflict pain on another.

15. *Don't barrow*—Not afraid of you.

16. *Boss*—Correctional officer, staff member in the prison system, supervisor of inmates.

17. *Chow hall*—Time, dining hall where inmates eat.

18. *Catch/katch out*—Leave without notice.

19. *Catch the square, katcha*—Go to a spot to fight.

20. *Catch the/katch tha house*—Go to your cell or prison sleeping area, cellblock.

21. *Catch*—A starting point to the fields.

22. *Come on back with it*—What a field officer (boss) say when inmates change directions working crops in the field. Pull what waste you got back, clearing the area of the waste you cut.

23. *Cellie*—One of two inmates living in the same cell.

24. *Clown*—Girlfriend, woman in prison, homosexual.

25. *Clauk*—Prison liquor (beer).

26. *Culture shock*—A particular form or stage of civilization with the surprise, horror, or disgust of the vital mental and bodily processes. Something you have not experienced or seen before.

27. *Chilling*—Setting back, watching what's going on around you.

28. *Chain*—On the bus home or to another unit or farm. A bus that transports inmates. BLUE BIRD

29. *Cross me out*—Telling lies about a person to hurt them or get them in trouble.

30. *Cho-cho*—Ice cream on a stick.

31. *Dog boys*—Limited that help maintain the upkeep of the unit dogs.

32. *Fly guy*—Cool inmate or one in the know.

33. *General population*—Whole prison unit with the exception of lockdown sea of solitary.

34. *Git wit/get with somebody*—Weak person, need a bodyguard, pair it up, two by two, go find someone to help you.

35. *Going to see Uncle Bobo*—Coming to prison.

36. *Get out of them/git out of em*—Strip search, take off all of your clothes.

37. *Head running*—Talking about anything and everything.

38. *Hat time*—What a field officer says when it's time to turn in from work.

39. *Hit on it*—Start to work.

40. *House*—Inmates' cell or living area.

41. *Hulled out*—Worked hard, tired, drove, worked extra hard.

42. *Ho-ass nigger/nigga*—Weak black male, like a woman.

43. *Ho/whore, ass shit*—Weak whatever you got.

44. *Ho/whore, ass laws*—Police, correctional officers, boss, staff.

45. *He's a (ah) broad*—Woman, female, obvious, liberal.

46. *Hook me up*—Getting a good haircut.

47. *hook up*—Connection, contact for something you need.

48. *Home boy*—Someone from your hometown, city, or good friend.

49. *It's on*—Going to have some problems with someone.

50. *Cell warriors*—Talking from their cell about fighting, only fight behind bars.

51. *Camping and tramping*—Sleeping in the ready rolls with all your clothes on.

52. *Click action*—More than one person fighting another one.

53. *Damn fool*—Don't care, crazy.

54. *Dog-eye*—To stare into one's eyes

55. *Dog boy*—Offenders who take care of the units' dogs.

56. *Don't make me dress you/yo*—Change your looks, beat up on one.

57. *Dawg (dog)*—Your buddy, a person you hang out with, a friend.

58. *Drag lines*—Strips of sheets or string tied together with a weight at the end of it and used to pull items to oneself.

59. *Drop me out*—Give me what you owe me.

60. *Droved*—Worked hard.

61. *Eats own*—Go to chow.

62. *Free world*—Outside the prison system, one who lives outside the system.

63. *Fight fuck or bust a sixty (60)*—An amount of money you can spend in a certain period. Fight or give it to him: money, sex, or both.

64. *Flip it over*—What field officers say when changing directions when working crop in the field. Chopping weeds with a hoe.

65. *Fell out of*—Place where crime was committed or where he was sentenced.

66. *I ain't trying to hear it*—Don't believe what you are saying or hearing.

67. *I-45*—Roll of toilet paper.

68. *It's on in your world*—Going to try and do you bad in every way.

69. *I don't borrow that shit*—Not afraid of what you are saying or during.

70. *Jail inside prison*—Solitary confinement for fifteen days.

71. *Jiggers*—Watch for police or security, correctional officers, staff members.

72. *Johnnies*—Sack lunches, is eaten when working outside the unit or cannot turn in for lunch in the chow hall.

73. *Jocking*—a means of positioning yourself.

74. *Jack mack*—Mackerel fish in a can.

75. *Jack Books*—Pornography, sexual excitement books.

76. *Killing*—Masturbating.

77. *Kid*—Used as a ???

78. *Kite*—A message or a note to another inmate.

79. *Layin*—Having an excuse on paper not to go to work

80. *Lookout*—What officers and inmates say to get your attention.

81. *Larson*—Hate in your heart.

82. *Move it around*—Go to another spot, any other spot.

83. *Mash tha/the gas*—checked, Leave without conversation, find yourself some business.

84. *Mask*—Making a hard-looking face, trying to look tough.

85. *Mark*—Weak-minded person and weak in body strength.

86. *Nah!*—No.

87. *Off*—To kill.

88. *Old thang/thing*—Have been locked up a while, no loved ones in the free world.

89. *Player hater/hata*—one who hates or dislikes people in the know.

90. *Pass*—Used to go from one part of the prison to the other, to appointments.

91. *Pair it up*—Get beside another person or two by two.

92. *Peep mirrors*—Small pieces of broken mirrors or a full-size mirror used to see outside your cell.

93. *Piece*—His penis.

94. *Pistols*—Fist or gloves worn by an inmate.

95. *Post her bitch ass up*—To kill on, masturbating on while looking at a woman or homosexual.

96. *Paper*—Money in prison, any kind of property that can be bought or sold.

97. *Pat Search*—search one's body by hand.

98. *Pin in the wind*—Write a letter or fill out a form.

99. *Possession and delivery*—Selling drugs.

100. *Pusher*—Selling drugs on the streets.

101. *Punk*—???

102. *Protective custody*—Locked away from the general population, alone.

103. *Rack time*—All inmates are to be in their bunks or cells.

104. *Roach*—Dirty inmate, will not keep himself or his belongings clean.

105. *Rolling Doors*—Opening of cell doors

106. *Ruffer bate*—Nasty person, can live or survive in a nasty or dirty environment or use things as he finds them. Reduced to less than a man.

107. *Riding*—Kicking it with your home boys about the world.

108. *Ride*—Made to go alone with the program or a person's program, to do as another tells you.

109. *Rescued*—Going to prison, saved him from his own fate on the outside.

110. *Runs*—Walkways on the wings or living off inmates.

111. *Stay down fool*—wood, fool, white boy in the know who will fight, fight anybody.

112. *Spread*—Mixing of food together by inmates, eating together like a picnic.

113. *Shake down*—Searching for contraband and property, body searches.

114. *Snitch*—Tell on someone.

115. *Shank*—Knives made in prison or a weapon.

116. *Scrub*—Nothing in prison, less than, stunted.

117. *Skins*—Rolling papers.

118. *Selling wolf tickets*—Telling lies or saying things you can't do or back up.

119. *SSI*—support service inmate.

120. *Sold his soul for a jelly roll*—Weak person who sells out for small things.

121. *Selling a hog*—Telling lies and inmates believing it.

122. *Shot of mud*—Cup of coffee, dope in prison.

123. *Stuck out*—Missed an appointment or assignment.

124. *Solitary confinement*—It's a punishment by lockup for fifteen days.

125. *Sweating me*—Working about what you are doing, working about your business.

126. *T. Jones*—Mother.

127. *Turned-out*—Made into a homosexual in the prison system against your will.

128. *Turn-out*—Going to work or to take care of your business, leaving your cell or wing.

129. *Turnkey*—Inmates who open doors for officers and inmates.

130. *Tuff Skin*—White boy in the know and will defend himself at any cost.

131. *Truck mail*—In-house communications, letters, mail within the system.

132. *Tight lace*—Free worlds, tailor-made cigarettes.

133. *Three hots and a cot*—Three meals and a place to sleep in prison.

134. *These thangs/things*—Fist, hands.

135. *What it is/wuz*—What's happening.

136. *Wrack*—getting into trouble.

137. *Welleso*—Punk, Chavpa.

138. *What's up fool*—Asking an inmate that don't care what's going on.

139. *Wham-whams*—Cookies.

140. *Writ writer*—Jailhouse lawyer.

141. *What's up*—What's going on or what you want to do, what's on your mind.

142. *Who you gonna git witt/get with*—Belong to a group or a person, choose someone you cannot stay natural.

143. *What's really happening*—Tell me the truth.

144. *Wire him up*—Getting a person angry to do something to someone else.

145. *Wings*—Areas where inmates are housed.

146. *Worlds*—Outside the prison.

147. *You ain't did it yet*—Stop talking and get it on, do something, let me see what you got.

148. *You better git/get somewhere*—Leave now.

149. *You better find you some business*—Get out of this conversation.

150. *You gon ride, are going to*—Get someone to take care of you, be a kid.

151. *You gon mind, are going to*—Obey the rules, do as you are told.

152. *Youzaho*—Short for "you are a whore."

153. *You are a trip*—Always got something to say about everything.

154. *You got that mack*—Jack mack.

155. *You are jonning*—Wanting something bad like an addiction.

156. *Zoo-zoos*—Honey buns.

157. *Nigger's piece*—A black man's penis.

The Keeper and the Kept

Any day on a slightly foggy morning between five and six o'clock, as officers report to shift meeting, they appear to be walking in a hypnotized state as they stroll into the building. As I approached the unit, maybe it's the predawn fog that makes the iron and concrete building look like something out of a horror movie. Maybe it's the way we all shuffle toward it like zombies. It's so quiet from the outside; it looks like it's deserted. But there are hundreds of people inside. Some of them will leave as we arrive to start our shifts. Others are never leaving. Some officers sit motionless in the shift meeting, almost mummylike, while others are talking and joking. Men and women come to a place most never want to think about, and we call it our workplace. I sit in shift meeting, awaiting orders of the day. The roll is called, and you are given your assignment for the day. There's a feeling of locking and loading, getting ready for combat, or going into a war zone. I turn to another officer, saying, "This is going to be a good day." The officers who worked last night look like hell, and they don't have anything good to say about what went on. I am having a hard time following their words because that voice in my head is back, and it's just about as loud as Crybaby's is on J wing. I ask myself, *Why are you doing this to yourself? Just turn around and go home.* But I've got my routine, and I just file on in like an inmate headed to his cell for lockup.

Now it's time to go to our assignments, and all you have to do is look at another officer's face to know where he or she is posted for the day. Mainly what you see is sadness or fear or disappointment. There are times when you look forward to certain officers getting a particular post because there will be less problems between the officer and inmate. Inmates look for certain officers at a particular post. Some inmates know what officers are assigned to a post by the way he or she walks or smells without even seeing them. The smell of your cologne or the hard heels on your shoes is a dead giveaway. Some inmates can and do count your steps and know who's doing the walking. An officer's mentality or personality dictates what a certain wing or **cellblock will be like that day most of the time. As staff go to their assigned post, inmates watch with anticipation as if they were the ones who assigned the officers to their post. Offenders separate officers into three categories of weak, mellow, and hard. Believe it or not, most inmates like a hard officer rather than a weak or mellow one because they know what to expect from a hard officer.

It's been a long hot, humid summer night but fairly quiet at the correctional unit, and the shift before you is willing and ready to get out of the building. The only thing keeping it from being a blistering-hot night is perhaps the coldness of the iron bars and concrete with an air of loneness.

The wing looks empty with an exception; sometimes there's an old two-by-four chair with a rag-cushioned bottom sitting just outside a cleaning storeroom, which the wing porters use for relaxing when not cleaning the wing. There were a few yells and outcries throughout the unit; most of which came from the dimly lighted locked-down part of the unit, administrative segregation. You enter the segregation wing or cellblock from the main hallway through a soldered steel door with a small slotted hole in the middle top half for viewing inside before entering. Immediately to your right or left, depending on what side of the hallway you are entering from, is about a twenty-by-twenty battle-scarred concrete room with bars and a door opening onto the wing runs with only a chinning bar and exercise mat inside. The general population's dayrooms are the same with the exception of a stainless steel combination commode and sink in a corner and TV in the other corner. There are about ten to fifteen iron benches with the seating capacity of about fifty and two to three concrete and steel tables, two and a half to three feet square with four twelve-inch round metal stools attached. Of course, these tables are mostly used for games and ***spreads. The dayroom in segregation is used for inside recreation only.

There are steel-grated steps just outside the dayroom bars leading up to the next three to four levels, depending on what prison unit you are

---

*   Cellblock—Sleeping area for offenders.
**   Spreads—The mixing of food by offenders, eating together like a picnic.

assigned. Looking straight ahead as you enter the wing, you see a concrete walkway about ten feet wide; and to the right or left, there is a wall of shuttered windows which are three or four levels high. To the left or right are the cells, which are laid out in rows three or four levels. Each wing has its own personality and so does administrative segregation. Sometimes you can enter a wing blindfolded and know which one you are on by the smell, cleanness, or even the conversation between the inmates. These wings are made up of five-by-nine cells with concrete walls and iron bars across the front. Inside, there are two iron bunk beds to the right or left at the front of the cell attached to the wall. At the back of the cell is a stainless steel combination commode with the sink attached to the back; all of which are bolted to the concrete wall. Also on the back wall is one light with a pull string. If you walk to the back of the cell and look to the front, just outside the cell is the walkway called runs. This is only about two and a half feet wide, just wide enough; if two people are going in different directions, one would need to turn sideways to pass. These walkways run the length of the wing with a round support bar about two inches in diameter. The iron bar rail is about three feet high. The administrative segregation wings are the same as the general population wings with the exception of the hard wire gauze steel mash welded to the bare doors and recreation room to prohibit inmates from reaching out and striking staff members.

As I began my rounds on the administrative segregation and general population wings, there was a constant chatter and name-calling. I never wanted to get into a mode that I have seen it all. I was also doing a follow-up on some management inmates in segregation. As I approached the wing or cellblock, it was surprisingly loud, and I didn't like this at all. The new female officer assigned to the wing appeared to be happy to see me, for that matter, probably any experienced officer. She stated to me, "What's wrong with them this morning?" I said, "They know that you are new and you will be tested. These inmates will talk to you in indirect ways." The next thing we heard was an inmate yelling to another, "Say, Short Dawg?" The wing officer asked me, "Who is Short Dawg?" The inmate was still talking. "Short Dawg, did you see that old uncomfortable builded bitch they had on the wing last night?" I told the wing officer, "These statements are supposed to **wire you up." She states, "What do you mean 'wire you up'?"

---

*   Wire you up—Getting a person angry to do something to someone else.

"He's talking indirectly to you, trying to make you angry." As we made the stairs to second row, another inmate yelled out, "You police need to get that old AIDS-packing-ass bitch off the wing before she infects all these old mark-ass niggers on the wing."

"Is he talking to me?"

"No, but in an indirect way making you the third party. He's talking about an inmate on the wing he thinks or considers to be homosexual."

"Look out, boss."

"Now he's talking to you."

"You need to check on that old suicidal-ass white boy on third row before he off himself. Y'all shouldn't lock a nigger on the wing with all these hos."

The wing officer and I began shaking down an inmate's cell because I had a tip from one of the snitches. These snitches usually have a motive. They don't like the person forced, paid, or threatened. When we removed contraband from this inmate's cell, he became angry and hostile as if it was okay for him to have these items. Policies mean nothing to some inmates. Some have been guilty of having in their possession things such as lipstick or silk underwear. For the record, you sometimes ask where they got these items from, and you know the answer: "I found it in the trash" or an unknown inmate gave it to him. Doing my visit to the wing, I had been asked to check on an inmate by the nickname Rat. He was the one inmates look for if they need something to be picked up or cleaned up for **paper. Paper! Ah! You are talking about money. You are learning fast. Rat's a white inmate about six feet tall, 185 pounds, with unkempt dirty brown hair, light brown eyes, and was very pale in color. He was twenty-five years of age, doing a ten-year prison term for arson and burglary of a building. He *fell out of a small country town. He was setting fires to buildings as a diversion and burglarizing another. Rat was the kind of inmate that will pick up and save just about anything he got his hands on until the wing officer did a cell search. One of the snitches gave Rat up on the cool, complaining that there was a bad smell coming from one of the wing cell. When I investigated, it was Rat's cell.

If you notice, most inmates or snitches will, most of the time, never send you directly to a person, just an area. I had learned in the past that even a

---

*   Fall out of—Place where crime was committed or where he was sentenced.

snitch has an inmate code for someone and has his own way talking. Rat had saved about fifty tuna cans unwashed, which he got out of the trash cans. No one knew just how he got away with all of these cans in his cell for so long or what he was planning to do with them, especially because he was in a lockdown status. There are some that take advantage of every opportunity. Some inmate had talked Rat into saving matchsticks and then tried to talk him out of them for nothing. Rat learned that there was profit in some trash in the prison system. Of course, Rat had pulled off one of the oldest tricks in the prison con game: by leaving his cell completely dirty, knowing that some officers will avoid it when doing a contraband search. Rat hung out with Tee Dawg; his first name started with a *T,* but all the inmates called him Tee Dawg because he hung out with Rat. I never did find out why Tee Dawg never got any segregation time after the fight he and Rat had with Crybaby. Tee Dawg was a white inmate about twenty-five years of age, five feet nine inches tall, 165 pounds, with brown hair and brown eyes. His large lips and wide nose gave him a different look than most white inmates. He was in prison for burglary of a building; of course, he had somewhat of a track record.

He's doing ten years also. He began hanging out with Rat to use or get him to do a little dirty work for him. Some said he also hung with Rat for protection. Rat would fight; he was not afraid of anyone. The word was out that the two together couldn't fight their way out of a paper bag. Somehow they survive from day to day, which was better than most. The problem with Rat and Tee Dawg was they always tried to con the big dawgs, which was probably more of Tee Dawg's idea than Rat's. Tee was more of a hustler or, should I say, an idea man than anything. Both of them got used most of the time. An inmate on the wing going by the nickname Crybaby was in segregation for fighting with Tee and Rat. He usually kept the segregation wing going most of the night with outcries from his cell on and off throughout the night. No one ever knew if Crybaby had a mental disorder, was stupid, smart, or just plain didn't give a damn. Crybaby was a very dark-skinned black inmate about five feet six inches tall, 170 pounds, twenty-four years of age, with stocky build, and large very round eyes, which were bloodshot most of the time from staying up late every night. His head was very round with short hair; his face was smooth and unmarked. His features caused him to look younger in years but hard. He had a wide happy-go-lucky smile, which he didn't show very often. I asked him once why he didn't smile often since he had a nice smile. He stated, "Because someone would think I like it here."

He's doing two to five years prison term for burglary of a building. Some that knew Crybaby from the free world said he started breaking and entering buildings at a young age. The grapevine says he was conned into criminal activities at a young age trying to help his **T. Jones, who was on crack. He was placed in segregation for fighting, under protection, which is called protective custody. Most inmates of this status have requested to be placed in protective custody because they are afraid or they have problems communicating in the general population. Some inmates would do just about anything to stay out of segregation while others use it as a way of life in the system. A large number of inmates believe that they have a better chance of getting what they want in lockdown. There is so much going on in the system with inmates jocking for a means or way of life. Survival is so critical that it becomes a market of its own to say the least. You cannot make a mistake once you are out there because there is no way back and another will take your place. Crybaby was more of a threat to himself than others; his growl was worse than his bite. No one knew if Crybaby could take care of himself in the general population or not. He entered the unit going into segregation for trying to strike a staff member. Some inmates will go after staff members just to get into segregation for protection. Sometimes just a slight touch from a staff member can cause an incident.

Inmates of this status are sometimes called cell warriors. They do all of their fighting from behind cell bars; they talk a good fight, but do not forget. Some will and do hurt others even through cowardice. Crybaby was usually speaking or talking to officers and inmates but most of the time, to imaginary characters. I think Crybaby enjoyed being locked down. There are inmates like Crybaby that try to keep some type of disturbance going to get the entire unit locked down. He would make statements such as he wanted a transfer because the food on this unit was killing him. He would tell other inmates that the food was no good and the warden was trying to kill them all and the security staff were killers and were ordered to destroy all the inmates. If his cell was dirty, he would tell the staff that they put a roach in the cell with him and he was eating up all his food. After playing this game for so long, he began to believe what he was saying. He was yelling to a boss, "Look out, boss, the bitch ain't looking for nothing but three hots

---

*   T. Jones—An inmate's mother.

and a cot. She don't even have a shot of mud. How would he like it if they put a roach-infested broke bitch up in his house? You see what they did to Short Dawg em, putting all them freaks on the wing, I'm going to tell the warden about some of you old gay-ass police he got working for him, Ain't none of you *hos* no good? All you hos like a sideshow like all of us are some kind of freaks."

* Roach—Dirty inmate, will not keep himself or his belonging clean.
Boss—Correctional officer, staff member in the prison system, supervisor of inmates.
Three hots and a cot—Three meals and a place to sleep.
Shot of mud—Cup of coffee.
Ho—Weak male, used for a little or nothing.

"I can't sleep at night. That old ruffer-bate-ass nigger upon three row got his dawg watching me all night, Ah, nigger come to the pen and can't get no sleep, I'm going to kill one of these hos before it's all said and done. I'm going to write my T. Jones and tell her all about this ho-ass shit you police mother f—kers are doing down here. Ah, nigger can't even kill without some of you gay-ass police just wanting to watch a nigger's piece." These statements were supposed to, and often do, embarrass the staff. This was a daily and nightly ongoing thing with Crybaby when he was alone in his cell. Naturally, Crybaby got his nickname in the prison system from his actions. He was yelling to another inmate in lockdown, "Say! Halfway, you wake? Have them bitches come down their f—king with you yet?"

"Nah! Damn fool, I can' get no sleep. You been selling wolf tickets all night with your old rescued ass, you and them other niggers. Besides, ain't nobody f—king with your old crazy ass." Halfway live on one row. He was a paper-sack-brown-skinned black inmate about six feet one inch tall with thin build but big bones. His once light brown eyes had a tired reddish look of age. His hair was long, about four inches, soft in texture, but thinning. He was about thirty-two years old but looked older. He's doing an eight-year prison term for possession and delivery. Halfway was placed in administrative segregation for threatening staff members, usually the so-called weak officers or female staff members. Most inmates looked at him as a pain in the ass other than being tough. Halfway usually made Crybaby angry because he never finished anything. He would clean only half of his cell or stop talking in the middle of a conversation.

Sometimes it would appear as if he had forgotten what he was talking about. He once pulled all his hair out on one side of his head just to get attention. He too, like Crybaby, had fictional characters. He would pray for you today and condemn you to death tomorrow. Halfway would become a different character each day. Sometimes he would be superman, a minister, the devil, and even a racist of another race; and he didn't care what race. Some staff members wondered if he had problems or if all this was indeed an act. I only had one thing to say about Halfway; he was good at whatever he was doing. Halfway possibly had a problem mentally, or he had a very good con game and would stop at nothing to convince the staff that everything he did was real. Most institutions have what they call an MROP program that is for the mentally retarded inmates. It's for inmates that cannot cope in the general population. They are slower to response to daily routines. There's an inmate down the run from Halfway going by the nickname Quick Draw. He was a thirty-five-year-old inmate doing a ten-year prison term for armed robbery. He drove the getaway car. Before he got caught with his robbery case, he was trying to do a little light pushing or, as some would say, selling drugs. He was about four feet eleven inches tall, 130 pounds with a limp on the left side of his body. He spoke very fast with a little stutter. He told me that he suffered his injuries from an auto accident that he staged to receive money and it backfired. So he ended up in prison and in the MROP program because he suffered some brain damage from the accident.

He still had the presence of mind to street hustle behind bars. Quick Draw was never a total threat to the staff as much as he was a problem harassing the staff. He would do small but deliberate things such as requesting to visit inmates in confinement, which is against the rules or policies. Once, he asked the warden if he could furlough or parole to his house because he didn't have any place to go. He would ask officers if they would drive him home on furlough after work. Before the system went tobacco free, he would ask me for cigarettes each and every day, knowing I didn't smoke. This was the mild side of him, the only one we knew until he was assigned a **cellie. His cellie was an older inmate, about sixty years of age. He was a very large man at about five feet seven inches tall, 275 pounds or more. A quiet and easygoing inmate, strangely, most inmates never gave him a nickname. They just called him Mr. E. Quick Draw called him Old Timer, and he was the

---

*   Cellie—One of two inmates living in the same cell or housing area.

only inmate to ever call him that to his face. There were a number of rumors that Quick Draw was a punk; others say he was like a son to the Old Timer. Anyway, Old Timer was doing about a fifty-year prison term, and he was not beyond doing a little homosexual activity. The two together had a very good con game. Quick Draw would get items from inmates promising to pay them back but never would, leaving them hanging. When they threaten Quick Draw, he would tell them that his cellie would pay them. When they go to Old Timer to collect, he would threaten them physically.

Once the cell doors were closed, he threatened to beat or punk them if they don't pay protection. Old Timer even intimidated some officers into not doing their duties. Some would overlook his cell when doing a contraband search. This was what gave Quick Draw the edge; some inmates thought he already had a good con game going on with the staff when all the time it was the Old Timer covering his back. Old Timer finally came to the end of his rope when he raped and beat an inmate close to death. He was stripped of all his property, most of which he had come by illegally with the exception of his personal items. Doing the investigation and at his in-house trial, it was discovered that he had hogged and bribed several officers and inmates into receiving and overlooking stolen goods. He was receiving sexual favors, bribing, gambling, and selling inmates; after his disciplinary hearing and the court date, he was transferred to another unit. Quick Draw had to keep a low profile to avoid the hit men, which took up most of his time. Now he was as quiet as a church mouse. I have been on duty all day and most of the night investigating a major incident. It was now about 3:00 a.m. on the next day or, should I say, the same day. It's 7:00 a.m. as I walked out of the Use of Force office after finishing my report from the night before. A shift lieutenant was calling out work call for some; most of the population had already turned out. As I got closer to one of the wings, I could hear one of the officers yell out work call. I and other Use of Force officers were well-known throughout the unit because we worked everywhere and, most of the time, into other shifts.

When I entered the wing to help out with work call, I spoke to the wing officer and reached out to shake her hand. When she reached out to shake my hand, she dropped her pen. As she bent to pick up the pen, an inmate took advantage of her posture and stated, "Say, dawg, this boss lady done bended over down here." As a male officer, you want to come to her defense but you don't dare say anything. Through experience, you know that the inmate is after you, but he is using the female officer to get to you. Earlier in my career, I made that mistake, and I paid the price. Catching me off guard, an inmate yelled to the wing, "Say, dawg, this must be this old boss man's woman down here. He is defending her." I always remembered that day.

Solitary confinement is only about a few feet down the hall. It is a form of punishment for inmates that have committed some type of offense against another inmate or staff. Sometimes they have committed gang-related crimes. Gangs are very popular in the correctional system. They have easy access and are used in any number of ways and reasons. Solitary confinement is usually quiet in comparison to administrative segregation. Some inmates have no intentions of living in the general population upon entering the prison system. They usually have personal reasons alone with their attacks against the staff and inmates. Sometimes inmates strike out at the staff to make themselves look good to other inmates or through fear of other inmates. Some just simply commit suicide. Some even go as far as striking out against the staff by not bathing, shaving, or requesting items they don't want or can't have just to aggravate the staff. The general population and some confined inmates have peep mirrors to look outside their cells into the wing or runs without coming out of their cells. Some of these mirrors are no larger than a thumbnail. Some inmates can see as far as thirty to forty feet away. They are oftentimes large enough to read mail or notes from cell to cell. Another form of communications of which they move contraband from one cell to another are draglines made from torn strips of sheets or string with something heavy at the end used as a weight. It is tossed from row to row or cell to cell, and items are tied to it and dragged back to the person holding the end.

There are shakedowns, and all contraband items are confiscated. And by the next day, it appears back in population. It is a revolving door, a never-ending battle. Just down the hall, one of the unit's lieutenants or sergeants yelled out into a empty hallway, which made his voice sound hollow, "Let me have all that kitchen and laundry." These were the inmates that cook the unit's meals and wash the clothes. I was called in early this morning, arriving at the unit about 2:00 a.m. As I walked out the Use of Force office after finishing some reports left from the night before, my eyes caught the clock. It read 3:00 a.m. As I entered the hallway, I heard one of the hall officers yell out to the wing officer, "Give me all of that kitchen and laundry." He was requesting that the wing officer turn out the kitchen and laundry workers. Most of the unit had slept like motionless babies all night with the exception of a few like Crybaby. As the doors began opening, the cellblocks came alive as would any large city. You began hearing large keys entering the locks of iron doors and the sound of iron banging against iron. Only about an hour or two later, you heard an officer calling out by wings and rows "Chow Time" for the general population inmates. As the wing officer and I walked the runs calling out chow time, the inmates sounded like hungry, angry bears awakened from a long winter's sleep. You heard growls and groans from men stretching and awakening from a night's rest.

As the inmates began to pour out of their cells into the runs of the wings, some appeared to be walking in slow motion as they make their way to the dayrooms filled with inmates. The wing bosses continued to call out by rows and wings chow time. Inmates began calling to one another from cell to cell and on the runs.

"Hay! Homeboy, is you going to chow?"

"Na! Dawg, I'm not going this morning. Me and some of my homies had a spread last night." Another voice rang out, almost like he was glad to have someone to talk to. "You and that old scrap-ass nigger need to get off the head running." Another inmate answered in an authoritarian voice, "All of y'all need to chill with that ho-ass shit and find you some business." Another inmate called to the wing officer in a light, requesting voice, "Look out, boss, you got one stuck out on two row." The boss stated, "He will have to wait for last call." Another inmate yelled out from the back of this cell, where no one can see him to the dayroom, "You ho-ass laws need to let the man out for chow now." There are inmates that just need to talk to someone. As I stepped on the wing to help out with chow call, I spoke to the wing officer; she dropped her keys. As she bent down to pick up her keys, one of the inmates took advantage of her posture and stated, yelling out to other inmates on the wing, "Say, man, this old man-looking bitch done bend over down here. These police sure know how to make a nigger's time hard. They know these hos are coming on to a nigger up in here."

I wanted to come to her defense, but you don't dare say anything. Through experience, you know that the inmate is after you but is using the female officer to get to you. Earlier in my career, I made that mistake, and I paid. Catching me off guard, this particular inmate yelled to the wing, "Say, dawg, this is the old boss man's woman down here. He is defending her. I have always remembered that day. The wing officers walk their runs in the line of duty, calling chow and other appointments; some are struck by flung objects from darts to spoiled eggs. For some, this type of contact could and did ruin some officers' careers. Some fight back mentally and sometimes physically. There are times when inmates turn officers against each other through lies and deceit, using them like pawns in a chess game. Inmates have gone as far as setting an officer up with the old respects con game by doing a simple thing such as disrespecting an officer they don't like in front of a well-known or respected officer. They start calling the respected officer boss when they were accustomed to saying "mister." Some officers have given inmates information about officers because of this type of deceit. Inmates will give officers nicknames for different reasons. Some given out of respect, but at the same token, some are disrespectful.

A great number of things happen on the wings for inmates that don't want to venture outside their assigned wing. It's where the meeting of minds and morals, the strong and the weak congregate. A place of recreation. This is the first physical contact population inmates, other than their cellies, have had with one another since ten o'clock last evening. As the wing inmates began to integrate in and around the dayroom, of course, there is some indirect tension, some walking back and forth like a caged tiger. As I look through the bars into the dayroom, thoughts run through my mind. All these men thrown together against their will give the appearance of lost lambs, but everyone knows within a few seconds it can erupt and turn into a nightmare of hell. But this morning, it is quiet with the exception of two homosexuals who begin hugging and kissing. Their faces already made up as if they are going out on the town. They are putting on a show for the other dayroom inmates with their painted faces. These two have not gained a position in the system yet, and this is their way of advertising. My mind is wondering again. *These people are acting like animals. What has our country come to?* The two, as many others, have been placed in a world of the unknown to some. Of course, men of this genre could and sometimes do take advantage of some situations as this, where there is a multitude of men that have been taken away from their female partners.

Most off the general population inmates do not care for inmates of that genre; a large percentage of these men have families. There are statements made toward them such as "You hos need to get off that ho-ass shit. Don't make me dress you up." Another inmate states, "What's up fool? That's my clown." The inmate returns with his answer, "I don't borrow that shit."

There is another call for chow time. As inmates enter into the hallway going to and from the chow hall and other places on the unit, the tension builds between officers and inmates, sometimes inmate to inmate. This is usually the first meeting place of the day for most of the general population inmates on the unit. The chow hall is usually the second depending on the time of the day and the activities of the day. Contraband and kites are usually passed from one inmate to another in the hallways, chapels, schools, chow halls, etc. Standing in the hallway, speaking with another officer about a incident earlier, and watching inmates in the hall at same time, I notice an inmate drop a piece of paper. I state to the officer, "Did you see that inmate drop that piece of paper and the other one pick it up? He's carrying a kite." As the inmates walk single file, you hear a hall security officer say in a loud voice, "Bump it on down, move on down the hall, stay in single file." Naturally, they will try and walk in the middle of the hall. A female officer does a random shakedown in the hallway that causes tension to the building and sometimes fights between officers and inmates.

Just down the hall, a fight broke out between Short Dawg and Rat. After the two were separated and an investigation was conducted, it was found out that they were fighting over an old gambling debt. The two would be put in administrative segregation for no less than fifteen days. The staff need to be alert when investigating these incidents because sometimes, inmates will do harm to the staff that come to restrain them. Often, these fights are staged. An inmate will often get himself put in segregation through fighting to get closer to another isolated inmate. He could have been threatened by gang members or other inmates to carry out a hit. Sometimes it is because he is a weak inmate or just in the wrong place at the wrong time. I came to know Little Mexico by accident. During one of my rounds on the wing, I noticed he was always staring at me, never saying anything. One day, he asked me to spell a word for him and read a sentence. After that, he began to tell me things about himself. Little Mexico was about five feet two inches tall with a weight of about 120 pounds. He had been known to be in the wrong place at the wrong time. He's doing eight years for delivering drugs. Some street people call them mules. He was twenty-two years of age with a host of sisters and brothers in Mexico. He had been in the United States only about six months before he got caught for the eight-year case. Of course, his native birthplace was why he was given the nickname Little Mexico by far. He didn't speak very much English and none at all when he's backed against a wall. He learned to adjust to prison life very fast. He had a look that could give you chills, but his body size said he was weak. But everyone knew to approach him with caution.

He was very quiet and only spoke when he had to or forced to talk. There were times when he wanted to write a letter but could not find anyone to write it for him. He often had other inmates write letters for him because he could not read or write that well; he appeared to be illiterate. Sometimes he would sit for hours, trying to find an inmate to read a letter to him. He would receive paper on his account that would be a total surprise to him. But the paper was not coming fast enough. He began to deal drugs and got involved in gang-related activities and other policy violations. Of course, he was the mule. That's all he knew, and with little or no education to speak of, that was about all he could handle. In no time, he became a gang hit man and would stop at nothing to stay in good with members. There are some fights that you know is a hit because of the way it is carried out; persons that know nothing of the victim carry out most of your hits. The sad thing was that Little Mexico became too good at what he did and became a renegade and was a threat to the gangs and the staff as well. Now the hit man became a target and was found dead, throat cut, face down on his bunk. But young Americans stand in line trying to get into prison and accepting jobs in gangs with no return or with death as the only way out. The prison grapevine says that he was Pen's mule before he became a renegade, and Pen had something to do with his death. Pen was one bad customer as far as I was concerned. Pen had no heartbeat.

Meanwhile down the hall, an officer IDs an inmate in the hallway for a pat search. "Catch the wall, inmate," the officer says in a loud authoritative voice. The inmate states, "Why are you stopping me, boss? I have not done anything. I don't know why you are sweating me. You police just want to f—k with a nigger this morning." The officer states, "Just catch the wall, inmate, and get out of them. I don't want to run my head with you." This inmate is now going to be strip-searched because of his suspicious action. A ranking officer yells down the hallway at an inmate, "Look out, old thang, get out of the middle of the hall." Without delay, the inmate rambles to the side of the hall as if he had forgotten where he was or supposed to be at this time. Some inmates are institutionalized from being locked up too long or, as some inmates say, doing too much time. They become part of the system without readily knowing it. They become a fixture because of their daily routines, usually by the way they dress, eat, or walk, etc. Raincoat and Big

Country live in the cell next to Little Mexico, and they are an unusual pair. Big Country is a white inmate about twenty-eight years of age; he stands six feet three inches tall, about 235 pounds. He has hazel eyes with brown hair; his skin has a hard, rugged look of abuse. He's doing a fifteen-year prison term for rape or child molestation of his sixteen-year-old cousin. He has a history of criminal activity in his family. His father and mother are doing time in the state prison system also. He has tried just about everything low-life at one time or another, from rolling drunks to beating up homosexuals.

The prison grapevine has it that he once made a state trooper swallow his chew of tobacco during a car chase and gun battle. He has an adventurous or an I-don't-give-a-damn attitude. He would do just about anything for a fast buck. Inmates walk around him for the most part because he has a hardhearted attitude and does not bar any inmates. This is not to say that he doesn't have problems. In the system, there's always someone bigger and tougher than the next. He also knows his place. It was once said he set a guy on fire because he called his girlfriend a bitch. Some said, but not to his face, that he is homosexual and his mother took his boyfriend from him who was only fourteen years of age. It's said that she is in prison for trying to kill him for leaving her for a younger man.

Raincoat is a tall black inmate standing about six feet two inches. He's very thin at about 155 pounds. He is about forty-five years of age with a prison term of thirty-five years for killing women; he says it was an accident. Raincoat has very large hands and feet for his size. His dark brown skin still shows a pronounced scar about three inches long on his right cheek. He always wears a large ring on his left ring finger that looks to be expensive, but everyone knows that expensive jewelry is against policies. Raincoat has the look of an old washed-up pimp from the early sixties. He loves to mingle in the hallways wearing a raincoat, which is against policies. One of the building captains gave him a job washing the dayroom windows in the hallway, thinking this would keep him out of trouble.

To Raincoat, this was like throwing the rabbit into the briar patch. Growing up on the streets made this act part of his life. Inmates such as Raincoat have been misplaced in society as well as in the penal system. The hallway has become his lifeline where he sleeked out possessions from which he survives in the system. He hangs around in the hallways pretending to be working, hustling cigarettes, cho-cho, wham-whams, zoo-zoo, and any items that are worth paper.

Inmates like Raincoat were one of Dopefiend's massagers because of his hall job and a need for paper. Most inmates like Raincoat were users or being used most of the time. Dopefiend was a thirty-year-old white male, three-time loser, about five feet nine inches tall, 160 pounds, with dark complexion and baby blue eyes and blond hair. It gave him the look of innocence with his baby face.

He answers to the nickname Dopefiend. He is doing ten to fifteen (can you believe it?) for possession and delivery. He has been in and out of trouble since he was a teenager. He's a rough, tough, scarping kind of guy that most people would like to stay away from because of his hard-core attitude. He was given the name Dopefiend in the prison system because of his knowledge in manufacturing drugs. Just as most inmates often do, Dopefiend had his problems when entering the system because he is small in stature and of the white race and, of course, that baby face.

When he's not called Dopefiend, inmates call him White Boy or Tuff Skin, which he earned. He is a likable young guy, but you know he is cold as ice. He has been put upon by just about every race of inmate in the system, and he survived by sticking back when he needed to or provoked. He never stopped to boast. There's a sort of code with inmates; if you fight back, you get respect in most cases, especially if you don't boast about the outcome. But by the same token, it could go on for days, weeks, or even months until one or the other gives in to the inmate law. The inmate code or grapevine is a good one; it never strays too far away from the original word.

It's hard to believe that inmates have a code of honesty. Dopefiend has a reputation for making some of the best chalk in the system. When he's not making chalk, he has a tobacco hookup. Some of these connections in many cases are renegade officers. Tobacco is a high-dollar item in most prison systems especially the ones that are tobacco free. In some cases, a pack of tight lace can cost double figures and sometimes triple. A can of rolling tobacco could cost even more.

Dopefiend is one of the few Tuff Skins to get total respect from just about all inmates. It is like being in the right place at the right time or doing the right thing to the right people. He hang out with no other inmate; most of the time, he is alone. He could take a shot of mud mixed in a number of ingredients, and some inmates would think they are back in the free world on Friday night. I am totally surprised that no inmate has died from some of his mixtures. Weapons and sometimes ingredients for Dopefiend's mixtures are easy access to inmates here because of the eating utensils and containers from which the food is cooked and held. It is easy to make battle and escape into the crowd. Debts are often paid in the chapels, recreation areas, and chow halls, etc., because of the large gathering of inmates. As they file from the chow hall back into the hallways, they look to be competing with each other, joking for positions at the pill window, which is located in one of the main hallways not too far from the chow hall. The pill calls are usually open during mealtime. To some, the pill call is their lifeline; to others, it is a means of profit and paying debts. The medical staff provides prescription drugs for the unit. Inmates sell prescription medication for other items throughout the system. These drugs are sold for commissary, sexual favors, gambling debts, and protection, etc. Some inmates even become addicted to prescription drugs and perform favors for the drugs, even threats and hits on other inmates.

Officers monitor pill call with strict attention, but some still slip through the cracks. Inmates will go to great lengths to hang on to their medication. The most common of all is the pill under the tongue. This technique is used systemwide, although just about all staff is aware of this technique. It is very important to most inmates to get medication because it is very essential to stay healthy in the system because only the strong survive. Some inmates use their medication as a way to relieve them from the pain of being incarcerated. To others, it is just another black market item. As the day goes on, the kitchen and the laundry workers are all now working on the noon meal and late laundry.

The SSI's hall porters and dog boys all have been turned out to work. The support service inmates usually support the staff such as cleaning office areas and places where staff members are assigned. Dog boys are assigned to keep the unit dogs trained and in good health under the supervision of a staff member; do you remember Raincoat, the hall porter? These dog boys play a very important role in the training of these dogs. They are not used only to track escape inmates but to find missing persons and detect drugs. It is now about 6:00 a.m., and the wing officers are now calling work call for the general population inmates. Once the inmates pour from their cells like soldier ants, they turn out to work wing by wing. The only inmates that don't turn out for work are the ones that are laid in for medical reason, court, or other appointments.

After a few months, I was assigned to the field force. Each field officer has about twenty-five inmates in his or her squad. I went to the wing where eight hos were assigned. As I called out the work squad on one row, one of the inmates on three rows recognized my voice from the time I was working in the building. Stating in a very loud voice, "Hay! Mr. H., why they got your old ho ass down here f—king with us early this morning?" I just kept walking, and a loud aware voice stated, "Spell *ho.*" An unknown inmate in a very loud and proud voice stated, "*H-o-e.*" I stated, "Wrong one." Another inmate stated, "Mr. H., you know that nigger couldn't spell."

There are a number of jobs to be done in maintaining a unit. Farm shops, horse lots, dog pens, hog pens, tractor shops, paint squads, yard squads, construction, and other odd jobs, etc. The fieldwork is the most demanding by far, but the work hours are shorter. This work can sometimes make a hardened, grown man beg. These inmates use hoes or aggie to cultivate the crops. This is backbreaking, thankless work, but it is essential for the functioning of the prison system. If you have never witnessed the field force turning out for work, it is something to behold. Some correctional units may turn out about two hundred to eight hundred inmates in squads of twenty-five inmates most of the time. Field officers go to the wings to turn out their work squads in most cases. There are times the work squads come off the wings at a dead run.

Sometimes they look like a military camp turning out for count. As they work their way through the building and to the back gate, once outside the fence or walls, we arm ourselves and count the inmates again. I call out to my squad, "Get with somebody, pair it up, get those hats off your heads." Hats or caps are not to be worn until you are on the trailers or at the work site. Officers call out their squads in numbers to load the trailers, eight hoe, five hoe, etc. There are about two squads to a trailer. Tractors pull sometimes up to ten trailers, which is called a line. A line could have as many as three or four tractors. After arriving at the work site, each officer unloads his work squad from the trailers.

Inmates are lined up and spread out by squads on the rows in the fields, which is called a catch. Orders are barked out, "Hit on it." Inmates begin toiling the earth, cleaning out the weeds, and turning the dirt over. It is a picturesque scene as inmates are stretched out across the fields that appears to stretch for miles. Almost unreal for all the inmates are dressed in white, it has the look of an old slave plantation from the 1700s. On a very hot day, there are times you can barely see inmates for the dust. As the morning goes on, you hear officers stating or barking out orders, "Flip it over," "Bring it all back with you." After a few tempers have flared and a few fights and about three hours, it is finally hat time. They turn in for the noon meal and do it all over again in the afternoon. After a hard evening in the fields, they turn back into the unit.

The first responsibility after a head count that the line does upon turning in is shower; that is, if there is not some kind of disturbance going on in the building at the time. As they shower under the watchful eyes of security officers, the homosexuals begin to make their move on the weak and the tired. This is only the beginning of some immoral acts of twisted minds with their painted faces, in many cases, home-made makeup. Some have entered the system as homosexuals from the free world. Free worlds are not usually harmed in the system as often as turnouts. Most cases, they do the choosing of a sex partner. There are some inmates that are threatened in some way and are turned out, which means that they are forced to take the role of a female in the system.

The inmates that are most vulnerable to this genre of person are the newly incarcerated. They are called Blue Foot. They are still going through cultural shock. If you fall prey to the vultures of the system, you will live a nightmare of hell. The homosexuals jockey for the rights to certain inmates by walking around the shower area with underwear rolled up and tucked in the cracks of their buttocks. Others keep a watchful eye for one or the other to fall prey to their immoral acts as the inmates make their way back to the wings in the sometimes-crowded hallways. After the evening meal, the challenge of morals, strength, and courage begins. As the night embarks on the unit, they continue to practice their skills of con games, buying, selling, strong-arming, and just plain stealing. The Blue Foot are sleeked out or put up on as if it was a way of life. When you put men of all races and backgrounds together, there are going to be racial problems most of the time.

It's raining today, and the field workers didn't turn out to work. I and other field officers were helping out by working to build security. The inmates and some staff members were not happy to see us; field officers are not the most popular staff members. We are considered to be hard-core and inconsiderate, eager to carry out our duties. I was working the hallway by T wing when a Tuff Skin about six feet two inches tall with red hair, blue eyes, some facial freckles and about 235 pounds entered the wing. A few minutes later, the wing officer called to me, "Fight on the wing." A group of Hispanics approached the Tuff Skin with click action, not knowing that he was not new to the system, stating, "Who you goanna git witt, white boy?" This time the group lost the battle. He dropped his property to the floor and stated, "I'm going to git witt you, Mexicans," and the fight was on.

The black inmates and some others cheered him on, "Stay down, fool." One group or another always goes for the underdog because this way, they can recruit and gain more control of the system. This incident has already turned into an opportunity for recruitment; the racial problems span from what group of inmates control the power in the world of the unknown. The mixed racial emotions, which are very easily misplaced in a prison setting. There are times when an inmate will have to depend on someone he don't care for or like at all. Some deep-rooted racial problems stand in the way. Some overcome this; others never do. Some inmates of different races that never before had any contact with other races become very close friends.

Sometimes even through protection, the immoral acts of prison life reaches out and touches some. This was a night of violence for an inmate with a prison drag name Little Mon Ma. I was one of the Use of Force officers; we investigated all the minor and major incidents on the unit. I was assigned to Little Mon Ma's case that next morning when I reported to work. He is of a biracial family; no one knows what race he really is, but he put Mexican American in his records. He's not a small person bodywise; he's about five feet ten inches tall, 175 pounds, and twenty years of age with curly black hair, hazel eyes, and a dark tan, almost golden. He's doing time for armed robbery. He has been in and out of trouble for years. He became a homosexual at a young age. He's not from a broken home, but it was said that his father was an alcoholic.

It was a hot night. Little Mon Ma was in his cell. Unfortunately, it was not marked single. Another inmate had gotten into trouble and was placed in administrative segregation. Unknowingly, he was put into the cell with Little Mon Ma. Sometime during the night, the incident or tragedy took place. A broken lightbulb from the cell was used as a weapon. And Little Mon Ma's life was threatened, and he was raped repeatedly. During the questing, sometimes I almost get caught up in the emotions of these victims of the con games or rape. Sometimes the questing can get very personal but you know it is your job and you continue.

Clowns are not given special treatment, but some are isolated upon request and at the systems selection to hold down violence. After crimes or violations such as this take place, the perpetrator is usually charged with rape as if he was in the free world. I have wondered what an inmate tells his family when confronted with the issue of rape charges in a male prison system. I guest most just lie. The first time I saw Sly Dawg, he was a clean-cut-looking black inmate, about 180 pounds, five feet eleven inches tall, stocky build, dark skin with a smooth complexion. He's twenty-five years of age and still had the boy look. Facing a ten- to fifteen-year sentence for car theft, he didn't look too happy. Once in the system, he was assigned a job as a wing porter, cleaning the wing or living area to which they are assigned in most cases.

His wing was laid-back; the disturbance percentage was very low. There are a lot of hard-core, free world homosexuals assigned to this wing. This turn of events was not to be at Sly Dawg's advantage. His T. Jones, his mother, was sending him all the paper he needed and then some. This could and did work both ways in harming Sly Dawg. In his case, it was too much money and not enough brains. A few tried befriending him to no avail. Sly Dawg was not a homosexual, but he liked the way the gays treated him and made him feel important or big in front of some other inmates. This is not to say he had any sexual encounters with them. The homosexuals talked after him, saying, "You are the man." When all the time they just wanted some of the paper he's getting in the mail.

Sly Dawg came from a nice family; he had little street sense to speak of but knew nothing of the prison con game. He's what the prison system calls a new boot, but inmates call them Blue Foot. He knew that he had to do something to keep ahead of the con game. He began gambling to keep up his image as an inmate in the know. His mistake was gambling with the heavies, thinking this would help him stay on top of the con game. One thing he failed to understand was that the con game in the prison setting is a continuous thing and the way of life inside the system. You don't take a day off, and you don't sleep sound.

There's a never-ending battle for power or control. Once you are in the heart of the con game, it is hard to get out, which he was soon to find out. In no time, he was gobbled up in trifling and trading to no end. The homosexuals had him moving and selling property all over the unit. When there was no way to his debts, the threats came on his life. Even the homosexuals began to call him punk-ass nigger and gay. He began to use the system as a way out of paying his debts, by signing up for schools, etc., to get off the wings whose inmates he owed paper.

He went from trying to con the staff to threatening to commit suicide. This became a pattern, and now the staff had alienated themselves from him, thinking he was only crying wolf. There were days when he was removed from a wing beaten very bad and hospitalized. Once he found that injuries could and did work getting him off a wing rather than getting beaten up, he could cut his throat just enough to be placed in the hospital. This became the turning point in his prison life.

Once he had been identified as suicidal and put on medication and protective custody, it was downhill all the way. He went from the hospital to rehabilitation to lockdown then released back into the general population wherein a few weeks or days, he repeated the same thing. He began to rebel and fight the staff saying that they were his downfall. He became a disciplinary problem. By this time, Sly Dawg had developed an appetite for the fast lane in the system, and old habits were hard to stop. In just a few months, Sly Dawg had managed to squander off hundreds of dollars inside the system. None of which was paid in cash because inmates are not allowed to spend cash in the system. He was the product of too much cash at the wrong time. Just in a few short months, he had been cut down to a bum or what inmates call scrubs or roach, whichever comes first. Some say the medication, others stated that it was a matter of morals that caused him to take the downhill slide.

When not in the hospital or lockdown, he would be seen in the hallways and on the wings with his clothes hanging off or walking out the back of his shoes and sobbing from the mouth. In just a few months, Sly Dawg had went from well-known and a likable inmate to a kite and jigger man, carrying messages for inmates and watching for security as inmates violate policies. He was slowly becoming the unit's ruffer bate, just a body, not recognized as much of a man. He even went as far as doing some snitching to pay off debts. It's like he had become invisible; he's not there or didn't have anyone who would befriend him. I asked him during an investigation if he had a girlfriend in the free world and what he was going to say to her about all the scars on his neck from suicide attempts.

He would just look at you as if to say "What do you want from me?" shrug his shoulders, and walk away. Sly Dawg had done some snitching from Boss Buster in the past; it is believed that Buster had received some bad tips that hurt his career. This is believed to be what drove him to become very vindictive to inmates. Officer Buster was a careless person and appeared to have something against the world. His young twenty-two-year-old stocky body and carefree, loose walk in itself were intimidating to inmates and some staff members. His demeanor often gave me the impression that he really was an inmate. But by the same token, I respected him because of his courage. There are some officers that try to do their best, but when put under pressure, even some of the best break. Not Buster, he is hard to the core without compassion for woman, man, or beast.

Buster knew that officers are struck daily by the hands or weapons of inmates. I never wanted to work a post behind Buster because he always kept the inmates on edge. There are times when I come to the end of my rope and strike back, but I always try to use some tact or psychology. Some officers lose all control and have been known to walk into a room of thirty inmates, pick out the one he is looking for, and hold court. It has been a hard, temper-flaring morning for the most part. Officers in general control these wings by their actions for that day. This was one of those mornings when everything appeared to be out of control. Even the officers were at each other's throats and the inmates sensed this and reacted. Even Mr. D. was having problems this morning. It was so loud and out of control I just wanted to go back to the Use of Force office.

Inmates give officers nicknames also, and this particular unit was no different. This one officer some inmates called Mr. D.; other called him dog but not to his face. Mr. D. had entered the system about one or two years before me. He helped me get through the first few weeks. Some inmates will help a new officer that they respect. Some inmates want to give you respect but not total respect; they will speak to you by calling you Mister and your initials. When giving you total respect, they will address you by your surname with *Mister* at the beginning. It had been a bewitched morning, and tempers were high on both sides. One of the bosses was rolling the wing's cell doors for lunch. This particular boss was given the nickname Buster by the inmates because he was quick-tempered and would strike out at inmates with little or no reason and was known to hurt some at times. As Buster rolled or opened his wing doors, he discovered an inmate holding or jamming an item between his doors to prevent them from closing.

I stood and watched this incident unfold, anticipating some kind of problem. Inmates do this on a regular basis, but Buster was at the end of his rope. The inmate law or system was winning. I was right; he was at the road of no return. Buster watched this inmate release his doors and continued to watch him from three row into the dayroom on one row. Buster excused himself from his cellblock, went into the dayroom, walked up to the said inmate, and began sticking him. Buster had been known to throw items such as boots, books, or anything on hand at inmates that were a disciplinary problem but never before went to this extreme.

He did manage to leave behind memories that some officers would fight back physically. In many cases, I enjoyed this type of action. It gives the inmates something to think about before attacking staff. I personally think the no-hostage law is best for all correctional officers. He was one of many that have been driven to the end of the line. Some officers have entered into a world of no return. They have not only introduced contraband into the system through favors but have become sexually active with inmates. This type of attitude makes it difficult for some staff to do their job well. But this is only one scenario out of hundreds daily. Buster had a reputation for being truculent all right. It was believed that this particular inmate was paid to provoke Buster. But for whatever reason, it worked this morning, and he lost his job as a correctional officer. Soon after Buster was let go, the word was out through the unit grapevine that Spook had done some snitching for Buster, but it was Sly Dawg. Some thought it was Spook because he was using Sly Dawg to get to some of the homosexuals on Sly Dawg's wing. When Bugger came in the unit, Spook then started hanging out with him.

My first encounter with Bugger and Spook was on the recreation yard. I was looking for an inmate during an investigation; there was a never-ending battle against incidents on the unit. Bugger was a six feet nine inches tall inmate, 205 pounds, with light brown skin, gray eyes, and light brown hair. He looked older at twenty-five years of age. Perhaps it was his height and his lifestyle that made him look older.

He's doing a ten- to fifteen-year prison term for his involvement in a car theft and chop shop ring. At six feet nine inches and 205 pounds, he had the looks of a professional basketball player. It was not to be; he could not jump twelve inches off the ground. He had no athletic skills at all. He acquired the nickname Bugger when Spook saw him trying to play basketball and falling over his feet and said, "That nigger is a bugger." Spook was a black inmate about twenty-two years of age, five feet six inches tall, about 150 pounds. He was clean-cut, dark skinned with a baby face. Spook was doing fifteen years for armed robbery and breaking and entering. He was a quiet, shy-acting inmate, but he would speak his mind when needed. He was a hardworking guy; he would tackle just about any job. He was very polite to staff and other inmates, but most knew this was not a sign of weakness.

His grandmother raised him for the few short years she had with him. He said he never knew his mother or his father. Spook was the type of inmate that could do just about anything that he put his mind into. He did not fear anyone, but he would always try and make a good impression on everyone. He became friends with Bugger after a brief encounter about the nickname he gave Bugger. That was a pair to see together. After a few con games and fights, the two were finally separated. When Spook beat a homosexual badly for coming on to him, he was always looked at differently. Spook had mixed emotions about homosexuals; some he liked, and some he could not stand the sight of. Bugger was only one step from segregation and losing all his good time. He began to try to clean himself up; he started getting very picky about his clothes.

It was very hard to find clothing for Bugger; his pants and shirts were always too short. This would always aggravate him because he was a nice dresser in the world. His height made him look older for his age. Even as a youngster he got caught up in criminal activity. He dropped out of high school in his sophomore year because crime had become more popular and attractive than education. He could barely write a letter without help.

What little mentality he had left, the streets had stolen all hope. Now jail and prison was his way of life. For Bugger, there were no tomorrows, no future, no God, only what was physically happening at the present time. The only life he knows was the living hell. It was like some are born in and from another life. Talking to Bugger was like talking to a six-foot-nine-inch-tall eight-year-old child.

Men influenced into turning homosexual in the prison system are considered turnouts. Some are used just to make a profit or, in some cases, for contracts. Kim was a free world homosexual that took care of his business. Inmates with record are usually incarcerated on drug-related crimes. Kim was about twenty-five years of age, 135 pounds, four feet eleven inches tall, Mexican American. He never appeared to be very strong physically, but he did have some good street knowledge. Someone in the free world, I guess a family member or friend, was sending Kim paper because he did not appear to be having any problems getting what he wanted to keep himself up. Kim hung out with two other homosexuals going by the name Tashsa and MeMe. All free world punks. The first time I saw MeMe was on the back kitchen dock. I was a field officer at the time, turning in a work squad. The reason I took notice was because he was picking up fifty-five gallon cans full of garbage and pouring it into a tank.

MeMe was bad to the bone. With his overly muscular six-foot-three-inch, 275-pound frame, he struck fear in all offenders' hearts that he took a liking to, most of which was unwonted to MeMe's attitude. He would threaten offenders and carry them out for sexual favors. He was cold and uncaring with his freakiest ways and nasty mouth. It was believed that he was influenced by Tashsa. Kim and Tashsa hung out with MeMe for different reasons. Kim was sort of weak mentally and physically and needed protection for which he paid Meme, and he could afford it; he had paper coming from someplace. Now Tashsa was a low-down dirty dog with no respect for himself or anyone else. He was about twenty-nine years of age and nasty looking. At about 110 pounds, soaked and wet with concrete shoes on, and five feet two inches tall black offender. Tashsa had very dark and hard-looking, bumpy-faced dry skin, which covered his long head.

His large round eyes were bloodshot and looked old. He was ugly and did not favor anybody. As one offender called it, he looked like a turtle out of the shell. Tashsa hated my guts, and he told me one day, "You think you are hot shit and know everything." Because I always used his birth name, not his prison or street name. He was doing eight years for burglary of a building. Tashsa was the fall guy for MeMe and Kim. He did what he was told. As the day goes on, you know you must maintain a professional attitude at all times because so much wrong is going on around you at all times. As you make your rounds on the wings, you know there are other offenders being victimized, but it's hard to find or catch them in the act because others are holding jiggers even with snitches such as See N Eye. Jiggers are a powerful weapon in the prison system.

See N Eye was a tall black inmate at about six feet two inches and 185 pounds, had dark complexion with thin, recessing, curly salt-and-pepper hair and very shifty eyes. The one full gold tooth in the front of his mouth stood out when he smiled. See N Eye was about forty-five years of age doing fifteen years on an involuntary manslaughter charge. His drinking was the cause of his incarceration. He hit a pedestrian in his car and ran while under the influence of alcohol. See N Eye always played the part of being intelligent, but he couldn't express himself verbally but took pride in being a good speller of words, which showed that he did have some degree of intelligence. He had very little or no friends inside the system; strangely enough, no inmates gave him problems. It appeared that they stayed away from him because he earned the name See N Eye because he would see everything and would do some snitching, and he drew a lot of attention from the staff.

In other words, he was too hot to be close to at times. He would snitch on some inmates and wait to see if they were going to do anything. If they did nothing, he would snitch on them to their supervisor. But what inmates didn't know was that most of the staff members stayed away from him as much as possible. I always felt that he had a knife in your back or that it could happen at any time. See N Eye once snitched to security about some gambling that was going down. When the inmates were busted, it was found out that See N Eye was part of the gambling ring. He then tried to sell an unverifiable story or hog that he was involved to get information for the staff.

After a few months, See N Eye was transferred to another unit, and the grapevine had it that he was injured badly by some gang members. Some said he was dead. I realized that this was only one out of thousands and continued to do my job. As all of the street and con games from different cities and states compete for power, remember, it's only a revolving door. What you gain today you may very well lose tomorrow. Some inmates are unique in these personalities; such a person was Dead and Gone, and he would stop at nothing. Some say he got his nickname from people on the streets in the free world. When people asked about him, they would say he was dead and gone because most of his adult life was spent in and out of prison.

He was a black inmate about fifty-six years of age, very dark skinned, five feet six inches tall, and about 160 pounds. His pronounced lean to the right side when walking would get your attention, and with those very long arms, it was almost monkeylike. His hands were very hard looking along with his rugged face, and those very piercing dark brown bloodshot eyes, which appeared to be looking through you, gave him the look of anger. Some of his teeth were missing and the ones left are deteriorating badly from neglect. Given a life sentence some years back, which he has paroled out of prison several times like revolving doors, in and out of prison since he was about seventeen years of age. He lived on one row, which he didn't like because he claimed it's cold and too loud.

He is the type of inmate who would con you out of your property and sell it back to you almost in the same breath. He had his way with just about anybody that's not of strong mind. He had a way of wearing you down and then taking you over. He had conned young inmates into becoming his kid like part of his family, but not without reservations. Thereafter, he would take all of the kid's paper and buy items that, in some cases, he would sell or give the kid what he wanted him to have. This appeared to be hard, uncaring, and possibly uncivilized; but it could be a way of survival for a mark. Remember, inmates are being bought and sold every day.

Just as you think you have seen about everything, you see an inmate with the prison inheritance nicknamed Mama's Boy, a five-foot-two-inch-tall, 165-pound, blond-haired, hazel-eyed white boy doing three years on an assault charge with a deadly weapon. He lived on the same row as Dead and Gone. The prison grapevine has it that he was given a light sentence because he was defending his mother from his stepfather. He had been in a small conflict with the police before, smoking some marijuana. The reduced sentence was because of the nature of the crime.

He had innocence about himself, but his scowling look could be frightening. There was no physical threat on his behalf to speak of, but he was the most pigheaded person you would ever want to meet. It was as if he did not know where he was or that he was incarcerated. There were times he would say things or ask questions that are dangerous in a prison setting. He only loved one person on earth and that was his mother.

Showing his T. Jones's picture around was not good; as far as prison life goes, he was innocent. He did very dumb things that could possibility get him killed, and he did not believe this to be true. He was not to change his habits or things he did in the free world or the way he did them. He could not comprehend or believe that he was under policies far different from what he had been accustomed to in the free world. He was what you call all book brains and no common sense. Everyone was completely overwhelmed with his lack of understanding. I always thought he was playing a role. Some inmates had the nerve to threaten him. He would say to them, "If you hurt or kill me, you will never get what you want." I personally thought some inmate would kill him just for the pleasure. There were days when he would just give inmates his property and say, "It is easier this way." There are inmates in the system that think it is easier to be kept by one than to be sold over and over again by many throughout the unit. Some inmates will come to a mark or a kid and give him a way to go, fight, f—k, or bust a sixty. As evening embarks upon the unit, inmates have jocked for positions throughout the day; it is now the final act of the day.

They continue practicing their skills of the con games, buying, selling, strong-arming, and just plain stealing. The strong has decided what to do with the weak, and the weak has come to a decision to become victimized or fight. There is no amnesty for the immoral acts of men with any shame. The homosexuals continue to indulge in their activities as if no one was watching them. The sun was dropping quickly into the west, giving off a colorful tone. Inmates began to gather in the dayrooms to be called out for outside recreation; for some, this would be their first time out under the blue sky today. Others had never experienced being outside since incarceration. This day, a group of inmates turned out that never before went to outside recreation. If not for the heroic action of one of the experienced officers, it would have been a disaster on the recreation yard this day. Several inmates had gathered in one corner of the recreation yard. It was all for some inmate who snitched on another inmate's brother in the free world. It was a well-planned hit. Half Pint's brother was killed in the free world, and the one who did it ended up as an inmate on the same unit as Half Pint. The hit was to take place on the north recreation yard; I was working the hallway at the time. Half Pint and some of his homies were to execute the hit that evening on the recreation yard.

Some other officers and I, being alert, noticed that some inmates that never went to outside recreation before turned out this evening. A watchful eye and crowd control saved the inmate's life this day. This is an ongoing thing each and every day; sometimes it passes without notice. If these officers' efforts go without notice or an investigation, another hit would have been planned and carried out; and perhaps next time, the inmate will not be so lucky. As the evening wore down, inmates relaxed on the grass and benches, weight lifting, playing basketball and volleyball, while others were taking advantage of the weak and the freaks. Some were indulging in homosexual activities and oral sex in the open as if they were in the privacy of their homes. Some officers became angry and out of character because it was their first experience encountering this type of behavior. As some inmates returned to their wings from recreation, they encountered inmates such as Spanky and Shorty Mack. Shorty Mack was about five feet six inches tall, 159 pounds, twenty-eight years of age, a black inmate with a body like a world-class weight lifter with the strength of three men his size. He was a dark-skinned inmate doing fifteen to twenty years for armed robbery. He was a two-time loser. He had a large scar on his left inside forearm that looked to have been an old knife wound some years back. Before he was incarcerated, he was a small-time street hustler and pusher.

When asked about his family, the response was "I have never had any family to speak of. I have been on the streets since I was nine." Shorty Mack appeared to be a likable guy. Living on the streets from the tender age of nine made him a hard and cold person. He would talk to some of the scrubs like they had tails. Calling to some inmate on the wing, "Look out, old snitching ass nigger, go git me one of them tight lace and some skins. Katch tha house on the way back. Don't make me put these pistols on you and them other hos." It didn't appear to be a very large task to get a cigarette, but when it is a tobacco-free system and tights are going for forty dollars a pack or more, it becomes a problem and hard experience for a weak inmate with no paper. He will probably perform a sexual favor for some tights rather than deal with Shorty Mack. Mack had went as far as blackmailing some Blue Foot into having their family send money to them in the system for protection. He would loan an inmate a cigarette or something of value, and when the time came for payment, he would demand the same cigarette or item back or the payment would double or triple.

Some weak inmates do fight back and win. Such an incident happened when Shorty Mack met his fate in a horrible death in the hands of an apparently paid assassin who afflicted multiple stab wounds and cuts over most of his body. Some say he got what he deserved; maybe so, maybe not, but he was just as dead. Inmates come and go from the system without notice, others you never forget. Pops was one of those inmates you never completely wash from your mind. Now Spanky was new a breed with his green eyes and very fine blond hair and a milky white complexion; his chunky body and fat cheeks gave him the look of a baby. He was about twenty-five years of age doing about three years for burglary of a building. Inmates and staff gave his nickname to him because he had the look of Spanky from *The Little Rascals*. For one reason or another, he became suicidal, which earned him the wing name Cutter. Spanky got into debt with the wrong inmates, and this was his way of becoming isolated or going to protective custody. If the truth was to be known, it was because he was one of the inmates that paid for the hit on Shorty Mack. After a while, it became his way of life in the prison system, his way of getting attention from the staff. He had cuts all the way down the inside of his forearm. Spanky would fake suicide at least twice a week. He once pricked his finger and placed blood on his wrist to look like a cut for attention. The staff again came to a false alarm. Spanky had a problem of too little at the wrong time. In some cases, too much support or paper can be just as bad as not enough.

Now Pops was a different story. He's a black inmate about seventy years of age, about six feet tall, 155 pounds, with light brown skin and straight gray hair. I will admit that I went Pops bond several times because of his age; at least that's what I tell myself. He's doing time for passion of drugs. He's in good health for his age and had a very young girlfriend in the free world. Well, that's the word around the unit anyway. Some say that she was after his money that he had on the streets. Most of the inmates began to assume that Pops had money because he had several businesses in the free world. The inmates at the unit gave him the nickname Pops, but he didn't allow them to call him Pops, that is, to his face. All new inmates would find this out fast; he would become very belligerent. No inmates ever attempted to harm him, but some would have liked to, I am sure. In a prison setting, it's like a bond or law to respect some all the time, especially if they demand it all the time. Pops demanded respect twenty-four hours a day; he got it, and the inmates that didn't want to give it stayed away from him. It's like a win-lose situation; if you beat Pops, you may win the battle but you lose the war. There were always inmates who were willing to fight his battles for him because they knew there could be a good reward. There were times when he would walk into a dayroom of fifty inmates and say, "I want to watch the news," and some inmates would leave. No one knew if Pops would or could actually have hurt anyone, but no one was willing to find out.

An inmate stated to me one day, "Boss, you know that old man could hurt someone and you would still go his bond." Most inmates knew Pops had money and liked to gamble. He also demanded that gambling debts from inmates be paid in full, and they knew this to be true. Pops was a lover of baseball, and there were times when he would be the only one watching the game in the dayroom. Pops had been known to use inmates like Pop Eye to his advantage. Pop Eye was short on brains and strength but had nerve. Pops knew that Pop Eye never got mail and he had no family or they had disowned him, so he became his family. Pop Eye was five feet nine inches tall, 125 pounds, and thirty-two years of age with very short hair, the Ivy League look. He had large very round eyes, which made his head look even smaller. He had a very comical walk with the look of a penguin because both feet angled out from his body when walking. Pop Eye was not a true troublemaker, but he could create some when he wanted to in the unit. Trouble appeared to catch up with him sooner or later. He had an aggressive nature without the ability to back it up. He would threaten staff and inmates to no avail but causing a disturbance that would get him locked in administrative segregation.

His placement in administrative segregation would give some inmates an impression that he was tough, sort of like a false statement to what he really was like. He's very thin, which you could see from his weight and height. His size enabled him to slip through the bars and on to the run, harassing inmates and staff. Even with perfect construction, he would manage to slip his head and body through the food tray slot. He could slip right out of handcuffs. During the little time he was not in lockup, he would get into trouble by creating problems in the hallways. He would climb to the top of the crash gates in the hallway, and it would take about two hours at times to talk him down. If you were having a bad day, Pop Eye would make it worse; and if you were having a very dull day, he could bring it to life. Pop Eye never wrote or received mail during his stay in the prison system. Pop Eye was the fall guy for Pops; he would take the cases for Pops when it was to their advantage. Inmates like Hollywood did not like to deal with inmates like Pops. Hollywood lived on two row with Preacher. He was assigned there after he got out of administrative segregation. Hollywood's a small-time wannabe-free-world street pimp that forgot that pimping was over as far as he knew it a few years back.

Hollywood was six feet two inches tall, 220 pounds, a black inmate, light-skinned; blacks call their color high yellow. Of course, Hollywood was given his nickname by the way he carried himself inside the prison system and in the free world. He always wore sunglasses, even at night, when he could get away with it or con the staff with false personal property papers. I never liked being in the presence of Hollywood. I think it was his old pimping attitude, or maybe it was the sunglasses. He had very fine facial features that indicated that one of his parents was of another race. He was very quiet, which, in some cases, could be bad. His attitude toward the staff could be taken as not good, but he always gave all staff members total respect. Perhaps he's looking for some type of weakness in certain staff members. I believe that he could have the mind-set to inflict harm on others if there was a profit to be made. He could threaten you with his eyes and not say a word. Hollywood was one of these inmates that knew the rules better than most staff members did. Later it was discovered that it was part of his con game toward inmates as well as staff. Hollywood would con inmates into becoming his friend, get to know everything possible about them, and use blackmail to gain a profit. He was placed into administrative segregation for possession of contraband, in his case, buying and selling an inmate.

Of course, this type of action appears to be barbaric and right out of the eighteenth-century slave blocks. To a person that has never entered into a prison environment, they would not begin to understand this type of morality. Homosexuals such as Kim fall victim to inmates like Hollywood. The inmates' communications are cut off from family and friends; they are alienated from other inmates and staff. It may seem hard or odd to say this, but some inmates would perish inside the system without people like Hollywood. He never took everything, only what was needed at the time. After investigations, it was discovered that Hollywood was just about as corrupt as any inmate in the system. According to the files, Hollywood would use weak inmates through some weak staff members or one who was sensitive to his cause or not aware of all the rules and policies. He had been traced to using in-house mail (truck mail) through some staff to blackmail inmates in the system on another prison unit. Looking at Hollywood from a fitness standpoint, he looked very intimidating, but he was not much on the strong-arming of inmates. Don't think for a moment that he did not have problems too. As we know, fate is going to catch you sooner or later, and Hollywood was no exception. He was clicked on once for taking an inmate's clown, using him, and then selling him. After his court date, he was transferred to another prison unit. This type of prison life appeared to excite inmates such as Preacher. He's a five-foot-nine-tall, 180-pound black inmate with stocky build and smooth dark skin and was clean-cut looking. He's doing fifteen years for possession of drugs and aggravated assault.

Preacher did not get his nickname because of his religious beliefs. He had tried every religious denomination known to man, and he appeared to have no true belief in anything but himself. Not well liked but respected up to a certain point, Preacher had a smooth mouth. He could talk or lie, whichever came first, his way out of just about anything. Preacher had a strange attitude toward life; it appeared that he was ashamed of doing time but not ashamed of beating inmates out of their property. It was like it was all right because they were convicted felons. It's like he had mixed emotions about who or what he was supposed to be or his part in society. He did not appear to be violent or stupid, but there were times when he would become enraged or uncontrollable. Preacher had *conned* or, maybe that is too harsh a word, I should say *confidenced* his way into one of the high-ranking officer's trust. After which, he became very arrogant, vindictive, and truculent toward the staff members. Preacher had become so entrenched in his new power he thought he had that there were some bitterness between Preacher and the other inmates and some staff members for that matter. He once told a high-ranking officer he didn't have to do what he was told because he thought that officer had his back. He finally came to the end of his road when he told the warden that something he was doing was not under his job description. He ended up in solitary confinement. Once released, he then took his place back in the system as an inmate with a lesson well learned.

Preacher met Magoo by accident in administrative segregation during a cell move. Magoo was in need of a writ writer, and Preacher told him about

Pen. Preacher said, "Say, little man, I need to tell you about Pen. He is a racist son of a bitch, but he know the law and he hate the police. He don't like anybody." I know Preacher was right because I didn't trust anything Pen said. Magoo was something of a cartoon character by his appearance, but he was a real man when it came to standing up for himself. He was about four feet eleven inches tall, approximately one hundred pounds, and between the age of twenty to twenty-five. He looked to be sixteen with no facial hairs to speak of and by his size. He was a brown-skinned black inmate with short hair, which was very light in color, with fine facial features. His legs were long in comparison with his upper torso, which was very short. His long arms gave him reach, which he used to escape from handcuffs when cuffed behind his back by stepping back through his arms and hands. He appeared to be double-jointed in the way he could bend his body. Inmates on the unit gave him the nickname Magoo because of the large black horn-rimmed glasses he wore and, of course, his poor eyesight. He was a first-time offender doing an eight-year prison term for small-time pushing. The reason for that amount of time was he had a long juvenile delinquency record. Magoo entered the prison system just as any other first timer or as any Blue Foot would, in culture shock. He too, like thousands of others, was exposed to the con games of the system.

The con games did not work with Magoo, not completely, that is; he was a tough little street guy that knew how to take care of himself, which was unfortunate for some. Several inmates were participants in the threats carried out against Magoo, such as fights, hogging, and cheating. The final act was when they threatened his manhood, imposing homosexual activities on him. The little guy went on a vengeance spree that no one who was a witness would ever forget. Under the convict code and jiggers, he was hard to detect at first mainly because some of the inmates agreed with what he was doing, and they didn't have the heart or the guts to do it themselves. He lashed out with a vengeance as if he was possessed in the way he went about his work. His assailants began to drop like flies in a matter of two to three weeks. The unit was in a state of shock and fear; even Magoo's cellie was afraid according to his statement, and he was probably the safe one in the unit. Magoo's cellie was so afraid that they were getting everything from commissary to a blowjob from him, and it was hard for him to believe that Magoo was doing this to these inmates. With a Jack mack can inside a sock, he managed to hospitalize five inmates that had tried to violate him; some were near death. Some inmates said it was like the work of David against Goliath. On that particular unit as rumors and stories were told of the little guy, he grew bigger than life as he sat in administrative segregation.

It was said after Magoo was locked up in segregation as told by his cellie Spider Man during an investigation. Spider Man got his nickname because he was a coward. When trouble starts, he would slide into a hole like a spider. Spider stated that he knew it was on when Magoo started camping and tramping. "Believe it or not, before this incident, I asked Magoo why he was sleeping with his clothes on. He always stated, 'I am cold, boss man.'" Oh yes! I know it's hard to believe that Spider was Magoo's cellie. Spider Man was made to ride when they came to Magoo, so he was no help. Spider said he knew when they (other inmates) came to Magoo with the click action that Magoo was going to fight, f—k, or bust a sixty. As you see or hear, the little guy decided to fight, and fight he did. It was told during the investigation by some inmates that Magoo never had the look of fear in his eyes or face. It was like he was driven by something. He looked as if he had no respect for life or limb. They say he did not talk or say anything; he just took care of business. Some inmates fight in a different manner and act as if they were born in the system or were incarcerated all their lives. They look for policies that have been violated. They are called writ writers or jailhouse lawyers. They go about their work as if it is a paradise or resort on a vacation. Some act as if they own the prison system, and we are to do as they say by using the law to their advantage.

This one inmate with the nickname Pen comes to mind. He was a writ writer that all staff members watched very carefully. I never knew Pen to be in the general population; he was always in lockdown. Pen was a forty-four- to fifty-year-old Hispanic, five feet ten inches tall, about 220 pounds, doing a life sentence for murder one. Most inmates like Pen hold grudges against the justice system. They start out to get their sentence reduced or an appeal, but they usually end up defending other inmates to fight the system. Pen was no exception. He had been known to write staff up for having one shoe untied during the serving of food. If a kitchen worker gave another inmate an extra slice of bread, he or she would be written up on a rule infraction. He also wrote the unit up because his food was too hot or they didn't have the right law books in the library. Before he was locked in administrative segregation for being gang affiliated, he was in the gang recruitment business. He was hard-core with nothing to lose, but he had a sort of quiet arrogance about himself as if he was smarter than everyone else. He was never associated with an incident, but you knew he was the instigator.

It was common knowledge that inmates who seeked to be gang members had to do different tasks; some carried kites and snitched on staff religiously. Some even had to commit homosexual acts. Hits were often put on inmates simply because he was where a member wanted to be at that time. Some failed to carry out an assignment. Others were hit because they were of no further usefulness to the members or became weak or unreliable. In administrative segregation, he continued to give orders and carry out threats against other inmates and sometimes staff members. He threatened to kill or have me killed one time because I would not take a kite to an inmate down run. Locked down in segregation, he became more of a threat to the system by writ writing. Inmates such as Pen cost the system thousands of dollars over a few months or years. There is an old saying that criminals learn from other criminals; I believe Peaches is one of them. The only good coming from a writ writer is they keep noncompliance officers within the policies. Some inmates called him or her Sugar Bear, but he called himself Peaches. He was a twenty-two-year-old black free world homosexual, six feet tall with light brown eyes, about 205 pounds, paper-sack-brown skin color. The thing that catches your eye is that he had a very good personality and was well-educated. With a bachelor's degree in education, I think his major was physical education; you wonder why he was in the system.

He got caught up in the system through a DWI and caught a manslaughter charge, which he did eight years. He paroled that eight but was still doing eight as accessory to delivery and possession of drugs charge. In other words, he was in the wrong place at the wrong time and was a former felon, and back into the system he went. Good with his hands, feet, and his head, he gave staff members as well as inmates reason to watch him. It was a little harder to catch him breaking the rules because a great number of inmates respected him although he was homosexual and because of his relationship with the staff. Most inmates would not attack him physically and certainly not mentally. If any of them did, they would probably lose and most of the staff would go his bond anyway. Peaches was good at keeping some staff looking good and in the spotlight with their supervisors by covering some staff members' mistakes or negligence from the internal affairs. Inmates would hold jiggers for him, sometimes all day; I'm sure they were getting paid something. There were times when officers would let him into places they knew were not authorized. Just about all the staff knew Peaches was doing a lot of trafficking and trading, but it was kept low-key. It was like he had the staff members in a trance or they trusted his word. Through all the years working in the system, I have never witnessed another inmate get away with so much through staff members. It was fortunate for the staff that Peaches did not seek to break too many policies. Peaches's parents had a little paper and kept some on his books. It was believed that his relationship with the staff was not of cruelty or deceit.

Peaches and Slow Mo were friends because Slow Mo had a clean hustle. Slow Mo was about six feet tall, 160 pounds, a dark-skinned black inmate; and he was about thirty-three years of age doing a life sentence for murder one. He had very short thinning hair, which gave him the appearance of being bald. He had normal facial features for a black American. His long legs gave his buttocks the appearance of being high on his body. He had large feet for his size. I'll say about a size 13, but you never knew what shoe size he wore because he never wore the right shoe size. He would wear the amount of socks it took to make a shoe fit. His job title in the system was bootblack. He shined officers' shoes and boots and helped keep the barbershop clean. When he was not hustling officers for anything and everything from cigarettes to cigars, he was walking the hallways hustling anything of value. Some of these inmates could make a profit out of how to drink water. Slow Mo would ask officers to buy their own shoe polish, and they could get a special shoe shine because the state-issued polish was not the best. He then would use the same polish to shine inmates' shoes for a profit. He would wear other inmates' shoes or boots to shop, shine them, and then wear them back to the wing. He had been known to wear some officers' shoes while they were off duty. Now we know why his feet always looked large and he walked slowly. He didn't lift his feet very high when walking; he appeared to be sliding, and that's where he got the name Slow Mo.

Before the system went tobacco free, inmates like Slow Mo had a good hustle. He and some other inmates had been observed taking cigarette butts from trash cans and off the floor, stripping them, rolling them in the covers from an I-45, and selling them to inmates. Coffee is a legal hot item in the prison system; it is used for just about everything, mostly for gambling at which time it is turned into paper. The buying of coffee from the prison commissary is legal, but gambling is against policies. And Slow Mo knew every con game in the book. Slow Mo also had a little side hustle with the

Blue Foot, selling them hall passes that he had altered or picked up where some careless officer had left them. These passes are used to move inmates throughout the building. When the Blue Foot got caught, he would just move to another one. After the system went tobacco free, it was very hard for some inmates to find any type of tobacco. For others, the market never slowed down. Actually, the tobacco market picked up after the system became tobacco free. Of course, all the tobacco then was sold on the black market. The Use of Force officers' business increased also. It picked up because tobacco turned into big business inside the system. It increased trafficking and trading of other items. Also, gang activity increased. A pack of worlds would cost about forty dollars depending on who was selling them. The Use of Force department has not always been in the prison system. It was introduced into this particular system in the eighties. It is monitored under federal guidelines but run under state laws and prison policies.

It is one of the most impressive departments in the system. We were asked to carry out tasks no others can achieve. We risk life and limb as we go about our daily routine of investigations. We are asked to go into areas of the prison system on a daily basis to gather information on major and minor incidents. It takes a certain kind of officer to investigate major and minor incidents in a prison setting. Ninety percent of the time, you have no cooperation from most of the inmates and some officers. There is a need to understand a number of languages, not necessary to speak them, but understand it and how it is used on the streets. And believe me, there is a difference. That's one of the things that will keep you safe and alive. I'm not saying there is no need for bilingual officers, which I used every chance I got. But they are not always available, and not all are street-smart. There is a multispeaking language called street-smart. Just as there is a body language, there is a street language, and if you don't use it in the right place at the right time, you cannot survive and reach your goal. There are times when inmates investigate you as you arrive at an incident. Sometimes you cannot isolate questing as much as you would like, and inmates will try and aggravate you as much as possible. There are statements made such as "You hos was not there when my homie got cut," "You ho ass police don't give a damn about no nigger," "Now you want to ask the boy questions and he is damn near dead," "You bitches need to go and find yourself a real job."

There are times when you feel like a condor, waiting to see if a hanging victim will live or die to write a report on the incident. You reach out to rape victims in the line of duty as if nothing has happened; you begin to think if this is normal. But when you save a life, you know it is all worth it. There are some inmates that will question your morals, character, sexual preference, religion, and education all in one demeaning breath. Inmates are now turning in from jobs, recreation, library, and other assignments. The unit's noise level has lowered considerably. There are still a few inmates with some loud conversations, but it is spotted at best. A few officers have gathered by the door controls, and a handful of inmates watch them as if they are going to miss something. Most inmates have a thirst for information, especially if it is about the free world. Some inmates appear to be trying to stay up as long as possible as if they are trying to hold on to the day. They know tomorrow could be painful and unpleasant. As the day continues to wear down, the noise level is now down to a whisper. It is like a miracle that an institution with this magnitude of corruption could be this peaceful. As the evening falls and darkness begins to take over daylight and the next day comes to mind, the still and quietness become frightening as to what awaits them in the unknown absence of light. We call ourselves a fair and equal society, but by the same token, some of our keepers and administrators of our laws should and very often should be the kept.

We have in most states what is called the death penalty, but some say it is not humane in today's society. But we leave them sitting on death row, punishing staff sometimes up to fifteen years or more. The prison system as we see today does not and will not work in its present state. We are only cultivating criminals. If the justice system is used in behalf of the citizens and not as a profit-gaining organization, perhaps some of our citizens would not be behind bars or there would not be so much child-on-child crimes. If we continue to hand over our world to our children before they are mature, then we are in far long and hard times. If we want to stop prison popularity, then we need to take our children back from the government. We as a society are more concerned with the rights of criminals than the future of our children.

Index

A

administrative segregation, 9, 20-21, 23-25, 28, 31, 39, 43, 50-52, 54-55

B

Big Country (inmate), 32-33
black market, 35, 57
Blue Foot, 9, 37, 39, 49, 53, 57
boss, 9-11, 22, 24-25, 29-30, 32, 42, 50
Bugger (inmate), 42-44
Buster (prison officer), 41-42

C

cellblock, 9-10, 20-21, 29, 42
cellie, 10, 26-27, 30
cell search, 22
clown, 10, 30, 39, 52
coffee, 56
con game, 8, 23, 26-27, 30, 39-40, 51, 56
contraband, 8, 15, 22-23, 27-28, 31, 42, 51

correctional officers, 7, 9, 11, 13, 25, 42
Crybaby (inmate), 19, 23-26, 29
culture shock, 7, 10, 37, 53
Cutter. *See* Spanky (inmate)

D

Dead and Gone (inmate), 46
death penalty, 58
dog boys, 10, 12, 35
Dopefiend (inmate), 34-35
drugs, 8, 14, 26, 31-32, 34-35, 49, 52

F

free world, 12, 14, 24, 35, 37, 39, 41, 44, 46-49, 51, 58

G

gambling, 39, 45, 56
gang, 28, 32
general population, 14, 20-21, 24, 26, 28-31, 36, 40, 54
grapevine, 24, 32-34, 42, 45-46

H

Half Pint (inmate), 48
Halfway (inmate), 25-26
Hollywood (inmate), 51-52
homosexual activities, 27, 48, 53
homosexuals, 22, 30, 33, 39-40, 42-
43, 47, 51, 55
free world, 37, 39, 44, 55
turnouts, 37, 44

I

inmate code, 23, 34
inmate law, 34, 42

J

jiggers, 13, 41, 45, 53, 55

K

Kim (inmate), 44-45, 51
kite, 13, 31, 41, 55

L

Little Mexico (inmate), 31-33
Little Mon Ma (inmate), 38-39
lockdown, 10, 23-25, 40, 54

M

Magoo (inmate), 52-54
Mama's Boy (inmate), 46
MeMe (inmate), 44-45
Mr. D. (prison officer), 41
Mr. E. *See* Old Timer (inmate)
MROP program, 26

N

no-hostage law, 42

O

Old Timer (inmate), 26-27

P

paper, 12-14, 22, 32, 34, 39-40, 44,
46, 48-49, 56
Peaches (inmate), 55-56
Pen (inmate), 32, 53-55
pill calls, 35
pill under the tongue, 35
Pop Eye (inmate), 50-51
Pops (inmate), 49-51
power, 38, 40, 46
Preacher (inmate), 51-53
prison system, 7, 9, 12, 16, 23, 25, 28,
33-34, 36, 39, 44-45, 49, 51,
53-54, 56, 58
rape in, 27, 39, 58
protective custody, 14, 24, 40, 49

Q

Quick Draw (inmate), 26-27

R

racial problems, 37-38
Raincoat (inmate), 32-35
Rat (inmate), 22-23, 31
roach, 15, 24-25, 40

S

scrubs, 8, 15, 40, 48
See N Eye (inmate), 45
Short Dawg (inmate), 21, 25, 31
Shorty Mack (inmate), 48-49
Slow Mo (inmate), 56
Sly Dawg (inmate), 39-42
snitches, 8, 15, 22-23, 45
snitching, 15, 23, 41-42, 45
solitary confinement, 13, 16, 28, 52
Spanky (inmate), 48-49
Spider Man (inmate), 54
Spook (inmate), 42-43
spreads, 20
street language, 57
street sense, 39
Sugar Bear. *See* Peaches (inmate)
suicide, 8, 28, 40-41, 49

T

Tashsa (inmate), 44-45
Tee Dawg (inmate), 23
T. Jones, 25, 39, 47
tobacco, 26, 33-34, 56-57
Tuff Skin, 16, 34, 38

U

Use of Force office, 27-28, 38, 41, 57

W

writ writer, 17, 52, 54-55